This book is to be returned on or before
the last date stamped below.

-2 JUL 1982

1C. DEC. 1982

25. MAR. 1993

13 MAY 1985

13. DEC. 1985

17 JAN 1994

3 MAR 1994

15 APR 1996

- DEC 1996

0 3 FEB 1998

0 6 MAR 2000

1 5 DEC 2000

0 3 FEB 2003

D0715891

Evans Brothers Limited

First published 1950 by Evans Brothers Limited
Montague House, Russell Square, London WC1B 5BX

© John Trevaskis 1950

Seventeenth impression 1973
Revised edition 1976. Reprinted 1976 (twice), 1977, 1978, 1979, 1981

Filmset and printed by BAS Printers Limited, Over Wallop, Hampshire
ISBN 0 237 29181 9   PRA 7276

Note to the teacher

This book aims at providing, for children in the primary and lower secondary stages, the essential minimum of punctuation required for all practical purposes.

It does so by means of brief, cogent lessons, each of which concentrates on a single 'rule' of punctuation. The application of the 'rule' is shown in two or three specimen sentences, which appear at the beginning of each lesson. The 'rule' itself is simply and briefly stated in bold type, while vivid illustrations help to impress it on the memory.

Thorough and comprehensive practice in the use of each of the 'rules' is provided in the exercises at the end of the lessons under the title **For you to do**.

The Revision Tests are so arranged that revision and consolidation can be systematically and conveniently carried out. After each group of lessons (with the exception of the first) two revision tests are given. The first test in each case provides mixed exercises on the 'rules' covered in the group of lessons it immediately follows; the second test gives practice in all the 'rules' previously encountered in the book. Thus, Revision Test 2A is based on Lessons 9–13, and Revision Test 2B on Lessons 1–13.

Contents

1. Capital letters begin sentences

The house is on fire.
We play cricket in summer.
Every shop is full of customers.

Here are three sentences. Each sentence begins with a capital letter.

Always begin a sentence with a capital letter.

This is a sentence and must
begin with a capital letter. ➡️

T/the girl went
to the cinema.

For you to do:
A. Write out these sentences, putting in capital letters where
   they should have been used.
1. many people live in towns.
2. he wrote engine numbers in his book.
3. ice cream is lovely in summer.
4. please lend me your book.
5. all the boys in my class collect stamps.
6. she likes to help her mother.
7. your shoe lace is undone.
8. big trees grow in the wood.

B. Write out these pairs of sentences, putting in capital letters
   where they should have been used.
1. the postman brings letters to the house. he puts them through
   the letter box.
2. the teacher was angry with Jim. he was late for school again.
3. help me to lift this trunk. it is very heavy.
4. you will find him behind the tree. he is hiding.

C. The words in each line will make a sentence. Write out the five sentences correctly.

1. tap   turn   the   off
2. in   she   London   lives
3. minute   a   wait
4. my   at   look   present
5. the   wipe   on   feet   mat   your

D. In these groups of sentences the capital letters have been missed out. Write out the sentences, and put in the capital letters that are required.

1. down the track roar the racing cars. the people cheer as the cars speed towards them. the blue car and the red car are racing neck and neck. they flash past. now they are out of sight. the noise of the engines can still be heard.

2. we could not do without coal. it heats our houses in winter. mother needs it to do the cooking. without it we could not have a cup of tea. trains could not be driven by steam. hundreds of machines would be useless.

2. Capital letter for I

I took my dog for a walk.
Last week **I** was ten.
He is taller than **I**.

Look at these sentences. In each of them the letter **I** is used on its own.

Always write capital I when the I is used on its own.

For you to do:

A. Write out these sentences, using a capital letter for 'I' whenever it is on its own.

1. i got up early in the morning.
2. He said that i was wrong.
3. He and i went out to play.
4. Tell me if i hurt you.
5. There seems no way i can help.
6. i lost my place when i was reading.
7. Neither you nor i can swim as far as my brother.
8. i am a big boy.
9. i ran until i was tired out.
10. i told him i was hungry.
11. This is how i do my work.
12. She laughed when i showed her the picture.
13. She and i are great friends.
14. i do not know why i was late.

3. Capital letters begin names of people

George and **Joan** went to the party.
My friends are **Jack Smith** and **David Jones**.
Brenda and **Margaret Harris** are sisters.

The words in **dark print** are the names of people.

Always begin the names of people with capital letters.

J jack and J jill
went up the hill.

For you to do:

A. Write out this football team correctly, putting in the capital letters.

jim brown

steve green   john stokes

frank roberts   philip dean   neil ford

simon davis   mark long   derek hirst   tom williams   peter hope

B. These girls are in my class. Write out their names correctly.

jane harrison	julie richards	teresa wilkes
mary goodwin	ruth arnold	linda fowler
jackie smith	helen farr	emma johnson
sarah hill	liz young	fiona grant
anne pugh	jean lewis	lynn james

C. Write out these sentences, putting in capital letters where they are needed.

1. When jack was ill, his mother sent for the doctor.
2. I saw mary and anne walking along the street.
3. I wish I could play football like peter osgood.
4. She sits next to lynn baker in school.
5. carol and jane went to the party with clare williams.
6. He raced frank and ted in the park.
7. joan is older than jackie.
8. andrew johnson is a friend of mine.

4. Capital letters begin names of places

Newport and **Swansea** are towns in **Wales**.
York and **Durham** are cities in **England**.
France and **Italy** are countries in **Europe**.

The words in **dark print** are the names of places.

Always begin names of places with capital letters.

For you to do:

A. Write out these sentences correctly, putting in capital letters where needed.

1. japan is far away from england.
2. The capital of england is london.
3. On the east of america is the atlantic ocean. On the west is the pacific ocean.
4. A great deal of tea is grown in india and sri lanka.
5. I should like to go to france and spain for a holiday.
6. The river tiber is in italy.

B. Here you have to write 3 sentences. Begin each sentence in this way: I live in. . . .

1. Write the name of the street or road where you live in a sentence.

2. Write the name of the town where you live in a sentence.
3. Write the name of the county where you live in a sentence.

We like **English** lessons.
French people live in France.
Many **Americans** travel to our country.

The words in **dark print** are made from the names of places.

Always begin words that are made from the names of places with capital letters.

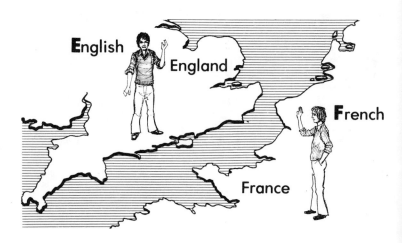

For you to do:

C. Write out these sentences, putting in capital letters where they should have been used.
1. Many sheep are reared on the welsh mountains.
2. The spaniards like to watch bull-fights.
3. A sikh often wears a turban.
4. At home we have a persian carpet.
5. Not all londoners are cockneys.
6. Many scotsmen wear kilts.

7. The romans conquered this country long ago.
8. The australians play us at cricket.

D. The words in Column 2 are made from those in Column 1, but are not in order. Write out the two columns, putting each word in Column 2 opposite the word it is made from. Remember the capital letters.

Column 1:	*Column 2:*
ireland	italians
holland	irish
denmark	belgians
poland	danes
vietnam	canadians
italy	poles
canada	vietnamese
belgium	dutch

5. Capital letters begin names of week-days, special days and months

Washing day is on **Monday**.
Mary was ill on **Saturday** and **Sunday**.
We go to church on **Good Friday**.
I went to the seaside on **Bank Holiday**.
My birthday is in **March**.
The first month of the year is **January**.

The words in **dark print** are the names of week-days, special days, or months.

| Spend Bank Holiday at **Blackpool** | **for 3 days only**

Monday, Tuesday and Wednesday at 8~30

Grand Concert |

Always begin the names of week-days, special days and months with capital letters.

For you to do:

A. Write out these sentences, putting in the capital letters where necessary.
1. The cricket season lasts from may to september.
2. boxing day in this country is on december 26.
3. On april 1 we like to play tricks on our friends. We call this day april fool's day.
4. My school has most of its summer holidays in august.
5. march is a month of blustering winds.
6. We say that april brings showers and may brings flowers.

B. The dates given in Column 1 below are all special days in every year. Can you find out what the names of these special days are? Write them in Column 2. The first is done for you.

Column 1	Column 2
January 1	New Year's Day
December 25	. . . .

14

March 1   . . . .
June 24   . . . .
February 14   . . . .

C. The names of the special days in Column 1 have not been written correctly. First write them down correctly. Then, at the side of each, write the date when the special day occurs *this* year. This date is different every year.

    In Column 3 write the name of the week-day when the special day occurs *this* year. The first line, for 1975, has been done for you.

1. *Special Day*	2. *Date*	3. *Week-day*
Shrove Tuesday	February 11	Tuesday
palm sunday	. . . .	. . . .
august bank holiday	. . . .	. . . .
ascension day	. . . .	. . . .
maundy thursday	. . . .	. . . .
easter day	. . . .	. . . .

6. Capital letters begin titles and names of people and relations

President Roosevelt met **Mr.** Churchill.
We saw **Queen** Elizabeth in London.
Earl Haig was a famous soldier.

These sentences contain the titles and names of people. The titles are in **dark print** and begin with capital letters.

King Henry VIII

Mr and Mrs Jones

We saw Lord Nuffield. ◄— Title with name—use a capital letter.

We saw many lords. ◄— Title without name—no capital letter.

Titles always begin with capital letters when used with people's names.

For you to do:

A. In each of these sentences a person's title is used with his name. Write out the sentences and put in the capital letters where necessary.

1. At the battle of Trafalgar the English fleet was commanded by admiral Nelson.
2. captain Scott died on an expedition to the South Pole.
3. We met mr and mrs Green in the street.
4. queen Victoria reigned for 65 years.
5. The duke of York had ten thousand men.
6. The Spanish Armada was defeated by sir Francis Drake.
7. The rev. James Hanson is our new vicar.
8. We listened to a lecture by professor Hopkins.

I hope **Mummy** will come back soon.
I went with **Daddy** to the pictures.
I saw **Aunt** Mary in the shop.
I helped **Uncle** Bill to mow the lawn.

Mummy
and
Daddy

Aunt Mary
and
Uncle Bill

The words in **dark print** are the titles of relations.
In the first two sentences, the titles are used *instead of* actual names.
In the last two sentences, the titles are used *with* names.

When titles of relations are used *instead of,* **or** *with,* **actual names, begin the titles with capital letters.**

Titles of relations
used with,
or instead of,
actual names. →

I had a present from Aunt Carol.
Mother took me out to tea.

Titles of relations
used alone. →

I have seven uncles.
Their mothers went shopping.

For you to do:

B. In each of these sentences is the title of a relation. Write out the sentences, putting in the capital letters where necessary.

  1. I asked mother for a pound.
  2. I went for a long walk with daddy.

3. uncle John has a beautiful garden.
4. I hope father will not be late for tea.
5. I went shopping with mother and aunt Susan.
6. We sent uncle Peter and auntie Janet a Christmas card.

C. In each of these sentences are titles of people or relations. Some of these titles should start with capital letters, but others should not.

Write out the sentences and put in capital letters where they should have been used.

1. mothers and fathers were invited to the school concert.
2. The chief of the Fire Brigade was superintendent Harper.
3. One of our most famous singers was dame Melba.
4. Three of my uncles took aunt Jennie to the circus.
5. I go to doctor Hope when I am ill.
6. I saw uncle Harry talking to daddy.
7. Three of my aunts live in London.
8. I know the names of all the kings of England.
9. I am going with aunt Alice to Clacton.
10. The two captains tossed for ends.

7. Full stops end sentences

It is time for dinner.
Look at the people in the queue.
We hope to go away in the summer.

Here are three sentences. You have learned that a sentence begins with a capital letter.

Always end a sentence with a full stop.

He closed the door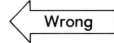

He closed the door.

For you to do:

A. Write out these sentences, putting in the capital letters and full stops.

1. the children went to the theatre
2. please show me the way
3. soon I shall be going home
4. all the players ran after the ball
5. it rained for the whole day
6. good work needs great care
7. look where you are going
8. next year I shall leave this school
9. once upon a time there lived a giant
10. write your name in the book

B. Write out these groups of sentences. Put a full stop at the end of each sentence.

1. The bus leaves the garage early in the morning During the day it makes many journeys Two or even three drivers take it in turns to drive At night the bus returns to the garage Before next morning it is cleaned

2. Milk is a fine food It contains fat and vitamins and other things to make us healthy We should drink as much milk as we can

3. Joe is very fond of reading Give him a book and he will sit quietly for hours He likes adventure stories best When he

19

has read about explorers or pirates he pretends to be one himself Then he has fine games with his friends

C. Some of the following are sentences. Some are not. Pick out the sentences and copy them down, putting in the capital letters and full stops.

1. she will not tell me her name
2. all the boys in my class
3. the last day of the week
4. lend me your pencil
5. four plates fell on the floor
6. everyone at the party
7. cook has made a lovely dinner
8. behind the cupboard
9. as soon as you have finished
10. hurry home to your mother

8. Full stops after abbreviations and initials

Mr J. B. Taylor has a case.
His train leaves at **20.00 hrs.**
Today is **Sept. 25.**

Instead of writing some words in full, we often cut them short, or abbreviate them.
We say then that we have used abbreviations or initials, like those in **dark print** in the sentences above.

Always use full stops after abbreviations and initials except:

a) when the last letter of the abbreviation is the same as the last letter of the complete word, e.g. Mrs

b) with abbreviations of metric measurements.

Remember, too, that capital letters are always used for initials.

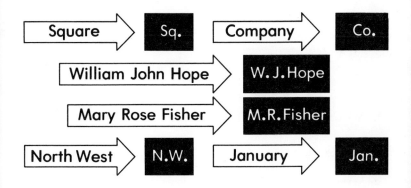

For you to do:

A. Rewrite these sentences, using abbreviations for the words underlined.

1. 60 <u>seconds</u> make 1 <u>minute</u>.
2. 1000 <u>metres</u> make 1 <u>kilometre</u>.
3. 100 <u>pence</u> make 1 <u>pound</u>.
4. 1000 grammes make 1 <u>kilogramme</u>.
5. 24 <u>hours</u> make 1 <u>day</u>.
6. 7 <u>days</u> make 1 <u>week</u>.

B. Write out these sentences, putting in capital letters and full stops where they are needed.

1. Mrs m e Hope sang at the concert.
2. Mr a s Scott is the neighbour of Mr b v Stanton.
3. My teacher is Miss l c Parden.
4. Mr and Mrs d g Smith live next door to us.
5. Thomas n Jones and David r Williams are friends.

C. Write the lists of week-days and months given below. By the side of each put its abbreviation. The first in each list is done for you.

Days	Abbreviations	Months	Abbreviations
Sunday	Sun.	January	Jan.
Monday	....	February	....
Tuesday	....	March	....
Wednesday	....	April	....
Thursday	....	August	....
Friday	....	September	....
Saturday	....	October	....
		November	....
		December	....

D. My name is Bernard George Hill. My initials are B. G. H.

Now do this:
1. Write down your father's initials.
2. Write down your mother's initials.
3. Write down your own initials.
4. Write down your best friend's initials.
5. Write down your teacher's initials.

Revision test 1

A. Write out these sentences correctly:
1. in the battle for quebec general wolfe was killed
2. the capital of russia is moscow
3. november 5 is called guy fawkes day
4. uncle bill sent daddy a new pipe for christmas
5. in scotland dec 31 is called hogmanay

B. In these groups of sentences the capital letters and full stops have been missed out. Write out the sentences and put in all the capital letters and full stops that are needed.
1. sarah walked slowly along the lane the birds were singing in the trees the young lambs were frisking in the fields the sky was clear and the sun shone warmly down it was a glorious april day
2. his mother told frank the way to go he must cross norton road opposite the police station at the crossroads he must turn to the left into gaton st fifty yards on he would see the house of dr williams it was no 36
3. capt harker lives in plymouth he has a nice house in staines rd his two children are named pat and sheila pat was 11 on march 15 sheila will be 10 next tuesday they both think english is the best lesson at school next year they will start learning french

C. Some of these are sentences. Some are not. Pick out the sentences and write them down, putting in the capital letters and full stops required.
1. the cat and the dog
2. dr livingstone was pleased to see mr stanley
3. george and sam played at leapfrog
4. through the window
5. mr gray always wakes early

6. along the river bank
7. when you have finished
8. there is a book on the floor
9. lend me a pound
10. tomorrow night after tea

D. Write down the words in the columns (a), (b), (c) and (d). At the side of each write its correct abbreviation. The first abbreviation in each column has been done for you.

(a)		(b)	
kilometres metres centimetres	km m cm	Street	St
days years months	....	Road	....
seconds minutes hours	....	Crescent	....
kilogram gram milligram	....	Avenue	....

(c)		(d)	
Royal Air Force	R.A.F.	Professor	Prof.
General Post Office	....	Doctor	....
National Coal Board	....	Reverend	....
Greater London Council	....	Captain	....

E. Write out and complete these sentences:
1. The name of our headteacher is ....
2. The name of our teacher is ....
3. The name of our neighbours is ....
4. The name of my best friend is ....
5. I have a cousin named ....

9. Commas for lists

Men, women, boys and **girls** are in the picture.
In the race are **Ken, Bill, Tom, Jack** and **Peter**.
Apples, pears and **bananas** are on the plate.

Each of the sentences contains a list of names in **dark print**.
Commas are used to separate the names unless the word 'and'
already separates them.

**When you write a list of names in a sentence, use commas
to separate them unless 'and' already separates them.**

> **Remember this pattern** ■, ■, ■ and ■

For you to do:
A. Write out these sentences, and put in the commas where
they are needed.
1. Mr Drake Mr Clark and Mr Hardy went to the office.
2. I saw Mary Sue Jill and Marion at the concert.
3. We walked past the cinema the church and the town hall.
4. I pass New Road Thornton Street and Station Road on my
way to school.
5. Worcester Durham Liverpool and Bath are English cities.
6. The farmer has cows sheep and horses in his field.
7. Mrs James bought tea sugar butter and cheese.
8. Chairs benches stools and settees are made to sit on.
9. We grow tulips roses asters and marigolds in our garden.
10. We need pencils rulers paper and rubbers for drawing.

B. Put each of the following lists of words into a sentence of your own. You must write 5 sentences.

1. plates   cups   saucers
2. knives   forks   spoons
3. buses   trains   ships   aeroplanes
4. football   netball   cricket   hockey
5. Africa   Asia   Europe

I sat on a **long, green, wooden** bench.
I walked through the **dark**, **quiet**, **muddy** lane.
The room was **large**, **empty** and **cold**.
My pet dog is **young**, **frisky** and **naughty**.

The words in **dark print** in these sentences are adjectives, or describing words.

When you write a list of adjectives in a sentence, use commas to separate the adjectives unless the word 'and' already separates them.

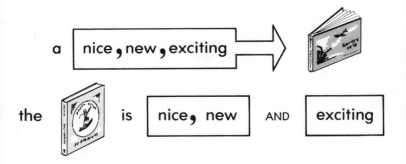

For you to do:
C. Write out these sentences, putting in the commas where they are needed.
1. I like English history and geography lessons.
2. The Union Jack is red white and blue.

3. It was a long hot sunny day.
4. Our garden is small pleasant and well kept.
5. The horse is a strong noble obedient animal.
6. Mr Toby is short plump and jolly.
7. A stormy boisterous wind was blowing.
8. She is a fine graceful happy girl.
9. His voice was loud bitter and angry.
10. The road is steep icy and dangerous.

D. Make up 5 sentences of your own. In each sentence put one of the following lists of words.
1. dark   damp   gloomy
2. merry   happy   gay
3. large   red   rosy
4. soft   white   silk
5. small   frisky   black

She filled the kettle, boiled the water and made the tea.
He picked up his pen, dipped it in the ink, wrote his name and blotted his paper.

Both these sentences contain a list of actions someone did.

When you write a list of actions in a sentence, use commas to separate the actions unless the word 'and' already separates them.

For you to do:
E. Write out these sentences and put commas where they should be used.
1. She ran down the garden picked up the ball and threw it over the wall.
2. She sealed the envelope stuck on the stamp and posted the letter.
3. He washed his face cleaned his teeth and brushed his hair.

27

4. She opened her purse took out some money and paid the baker.
5. I ran home from school had my tea and went to the pictures.
6. He sat by the fire opened a book and started to read.

She ran from the house **,** jumped on her bicycle and rode away **.**

F. Below are eight lists of sentences. Join the sentences in each list into one long sentence like those you have written in Exercise **E.** Put in commas where they are needed. You must write eight long sentences.

1. He walked to the door. He rang the bell. He waited.
2. He lifted the sack. He slung it over his shoulder. He walked away.
3. She lay down. She closed her eyes. She went to sleep.
4. Mother scraped the potatoes. She cut them up. She put them in a saucepan.
5. The guard looked at his watch. He blew his whistle. He waved his flag.
6. The grocer wrapped up the packet. He tied it with string. He gave it to the customer.
7. Mary pulled back the curtains. She opened the windows. She leaned out.
8. Mother put up the line. She pegged out the clothes. She left them to dry.

10. Commas to separate the names of people spoken to

Hullo, **Mary,** I have been waiting for you.
I will show you my engine, **Jim**.
Jack, please lend me your book.

The words in **dark print** are the names of people spoken to.

Commas are used to separate the names from the rest of the sentence.

Please pass the salt, Steve.
Wait, Steve, while I dress.
Steve, come and do the washing-up.

Steve is spoken to in each sentence. **Commas are used.**

Linda went for a walk.
I saw Linda in the shop.
I walked home with Linda.

Linda is not spoken to in any sentence. **Commas are not used.**

For you to do:

A. In each of these sentences someone is spoken to. Write out the sentences and put in the commas that are needed.
1. Please Mother give me some jam.
2. There are lots of pictures in your book Anne.
3. Bob your button is undone.
4. Goodbye Clare I have to go now.
5. Hello Jenny you do look pale.
6. Michael put that knife down at once.
7. I saw you take my ball Tim.
8. I can take you to Ian Alison.

9. Philip here is someone to see you.
10. I am sorry I cannot help you Joe.

B. In some of these sentences someone is spoken to. In others
no one is spoken to. Write the sentences out, and use
commas where they are needed.
1. Jackie sent me a birthday card.
2. Hello Sue I thought you were lost.
3. David your father is calling you.
4. I know that Stephen has gone Ken.
5. I saw Joanne going to school.
6. Many kings of England have been called Henry.
7. Peter tell Sarah I want her.
8. I think Jeff will be away a long time.
9. Anne and Julie are great friends.
10. Mind you keep your books neatly Tony.

11. Commas in dates and addresses

Napoleon was born on **15 August, 1769**.
He died on **May 5th, 1821**.
They spent their holidays at **Blackpool, Lancashire**.
I live in **High Street, Birmingham.**
She was married on **16 June 1975**.

In these sentences dates and addresses are in **dark print**.

In dates:
Either July 1949 *or* July, 1949.

Either 23 July, 1949 *or* July 23, 1949 *or* 23 July 1949.

In addresses:
Use a comma between the number (or name) of the house and the name of the street: The Pines, High Street.
Use a comma between the names of the street and the town:
High Street, Bath.
Use a comma between the names of the town and the county:
Bath, Avon.
Use a comma between the names of the county and the country:
Avon, England.

For you to do:
A. Write out these sentences, and put in commas where they should be used.
1. We live at 36 Windmill Lane.
2. I spent the whole of August 1974 at camp.
3. The First World War ended on 11 November 1918.
4. Nearly 90 000 people live at Ipswich Suffolk.
5. He has a job at Dover Kent.
6. He was born on February 16 1945.
7. He lives in Station Street Plymouth.
8. There were terrible snow storms in January 1947.
9. He will be fifteen on 9 December 1976.
10. Their house is The Firs Field Avenue.

B. Do these six things.
1. Write in full your own address.
2. Write in full the address of your school.
3. Write in full the address of your best friend.
4. Write today's date.
5. Write the date of your birthday this year.
6. Write the date when this term started.

C. A short way of writing the date is this: 5.1.75
The first figure shows the day. The second figure shows the month. The third figure shows the year.
5.1.75 is 5 January, 1975 *or* January 5, 1975 *or* 5 January 1975.

Write out the dates below in full, each one in two ways. The first is done for you.

8.4.76   *8 April, 1976*
          April 8, 1976

19.12.68	4.8.74 ....
6.7.42	17.2.39 ....
23.1.55	30.9.67 ....
28.10.27	11.5.19 ....
	15.11.43 ....

D. Find out in which country each of the towns below is. Then write down the name of the town and its country. The first is done for you.

Town		*Town*	
1. Tokyo	*Tokyo, Japan*	6. Rome	....
2. Paris	....	7. Cairo	....
3. Madrid	....	8. Canberra	....
4. Berlin	....	9. Dublin	....
5. Edinburgh	....	10. Wellington	....

12. Commas used in joining sentences (1)

He leapt over the hedge. He raced across the field.
Leaping over the hedge, **he** raced across the field.

She seized her hat. She ran out of the house.
Seizing her hat, **she** ran out of the house.

Here is one way of joining two sentences. The changes that have to be made are shown in **dark print**.

When the two sentences are joined in this way, a comma is put between them.

For you to do:

A. Write out these sentences, and put a comma in each where it is needed.

1. Opening the door he invited the stranger to enter.
2. Having eaten his dinner he helped to wash up.
3. Exhausted after his long run he lay down to rest.
4. Being the first to arrive he sat down in the front row.
5. Catching sight of me in the street he crossed over to speak.
6. Taking off his shoes he tip-toed into the room.
7. Racing madly along he managed to catch his friend.
8. Frightened by the noise the mouse ran into its hole.
9. Having washed his face he brushed his hair.
10. Having been asked to read he stood up.

B. Join each pair of sentences as you have been shown above. Remember to use a comma where it is needed.

1. He stopped behind a bush. He watched the thieves open the window.
2. He had finished his sums. He read a library book.
3. He was the tallest of them all. He stood at the back.
4. He ran to the end of the next road. He just caught a bus.
5. The burglar was surprised by a policeman. He escaped through the window.
6. He walked as fast as he could. He reached home in ten minutes.
7. He had put on his coat. He looked for his hat.
8. He peered through the fog. He saw the house.
9. He was tired of being alone. He went out to find his friend.
10. He had been on an errand. He was late for school.

13. Commas used in joining sentences (2)

The Amazon is in S. America. **It is** the longest river in the world
The Amazon, the longest river in the world, is in S. America.

Jim Jones is in my class. **He is** captain of the football team.
Jim Jones, captain of the football team, is in my class.

Here is another way of joining two sentences. The first sentence is split into two parts. The second sentence is put between the two parts. The words in **dark print** are missed out of the first sentence.

When two sentences are joined in this way, two commas are used to separate them.

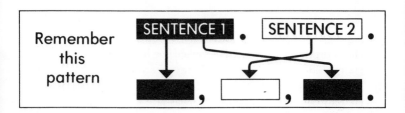

For you to do:

A. Write out these sentences. In each put two commas where they should be used.

1. London the capital of Great Britain is one of the largest cities in the world.
2. Radio a wonderful modern invention can today be found in nearly every home.
3. Charles Dickens a famous author wrote many novels.
4. Gibraltar the key to the Mediterranean lies at the south of Spain.
5. Colin Bell a well-known footballer has played for England many times.
6. History my favourite lesson at school concerns how people lived in the past.
7. The elephant one of the largest of animals has a trunk and tusks.
8. Franklin D. Roosevelt a former President of the U.S.A. was a great friend of Britain.
9. Ben Nevis the highest mountain in Great Britain is in Scotland.
10. The Bible the most famous of all books is a collection of many books.

B. Join each pair of sentences in the way you have been shown above. Remember to use commas where they are needed.

1. Rome is the capital of Italy. It is the home of the Pope.
2. The Thames flows through London. It is England's best known river.
3. Beethoven was born in Germany. He was a great composer.
4. The camel can go for days without water. It is known as the ship of the desert.
5. Grapes are grown in France. They are a delicious fruit.

C. Each phrase in Column 2 tells you something about one name in Column 1. Write 5 sentences, each starting with a name from Column 1, continuing with a phrase from Column 2, and finishing in any way that you can.

The first is done for you below.

Column 1	Column 2
Richie Benaud	a famous Australian cricketer
Blackpool	a favourite pantomime
Big Ben	the home of golf
Scotland	the author of wonderful fairy stories
Napoleon	an English holiday resort
Mother Goose	a famous French general
Hans Andersen	a famous clock

Richie Benaud, a famous Australian cricketer, played in England many times.

Revision test 2A

A. The commas have been left out of these sentences. Write out the sentences, and put in the commas that are required.

1. I hope Janet that you will be better tomorrow.
2. John Keats the writer of many great poems died at the age of 26.
3. I went with Jack Jim Frank and Sam to the pictures.
4. Mr Jones was 50 on 25 March 1975.
5. Closing his book he began to write.
6. The kangaroo a curious animal lives in Australia.
7. When I grow up I want to be an engine driver.
8. My dog a black and white fox terrier follows me everywhere.
9. Having sharpened my knife I cut a thick stick.
10. He opened his eyes stretched his arms and yawned.

B. Join each pair of sentences to make one sentence, taking care to put commas in the correct places.

1. Jerusalem is in Palestine. It is the Holy City.
2. He crept to the window. He peered out.
3. I struck a match. I lit the fire.
4. Robert Louis Stevenson was born in Scotland. He was the author of many fine adventure stories.
5. Hollywood is in America. It is famous for its films.
6. He opened his bag. He took out a bottle.
7. Sir Winston Churchill wrote many books. He was a famous Englishman.
8. I had been told he would come. I waited for him.
9. India is a huge country. It is the home of the tiger.
10. I mended the puncture. I went for a ride.

Revision test 2B

In these groups of sentences, no capital letters or punctuation marks have been used. Write out the sentences correctly, putting in all capital letters, full stops and commas that are needed.

1. marco polo a famous explorer travelled across europe russia and siberia to reach china when he returned to his home in venice he told wonderful stories of the things he had seen

2. i should like to go for a ride on my bicycle tomorrow mother ken raymond and i want to visit dudley castle mr smith our teacher says a fine zoo is there we shall see lions tigers elephants monkeys and many other animals

3. on tuesday and wednesday next week a bazaar is being held at school on tuesday april 18 the rev j n hope is opening the bazaar on wednesday capt arthur williams m p for camford will open the bazaar present prizes to the children and autograph our books

4. mr fisher lives at 53 trent terrace goldstone mr baker lives at 49 mostyn st goldstone on the morning of may 17 1948 they met at the corner of grange road and high street mr fisher a post office clerk was hurrying to work mr baker was carrying a basket of eggs tomatoes potatoes and buns they collided when mr baker saw his eggs lying smashed in the road he was angry he put down his basket took off his jacket rolled up his sleeves and wanted to fight mr fisher luckily p c johnson was near seeing what had happened he hurried to stop any trouble mr baker grumbled rolled down his sleeves and put on his jacket mr fisher and the policeman collected what they could and put tomatoes potatoes and buns back in the basket still grumbling mr baker went back to mostyn street and mr fisher hurried on again to work laughing quietly p c johnson watched them go

14. The possessive 's

Table 1

the **boy's** dog	means	the dog belonging to the **boy**.
the **teacher's** desk	means	the desk belonging to the **teacher**.
Mr Jones's shop	means	the shop belonging to **Mr Jones**.

The phrases in the left column are those we usually use. When we write these phrases we must use the possessive 's. The phrases in the right column tell us where to put the 's.

Look at the words in **dark print** in the right column. The same words, also in **dark print**, are in the left column.

They tell us about: ONE boy, ONE teacher, ONE Mr Jones. 's is added to these words.

Table 2

the **birds'** eggs	means	the eggs belonging to the **birds**.
the **ladies'** shoes	means	the shoes belonging to the **ladies**.
the **boys'** books	means	the books belonging to the **boys**.

In this table, the words in **dark print** end in —s, and they all mean more than ONE: many birds, several ladies, dozens of boys.

When we write the phrases in the left column, we add only the apostrophe, because the words already end in —s.

For you to do:
A. Write out these sentences and put in the apostrophe where it is needed.
 1. Dereks mother brought him to school.
 2. My two brothers names are Robert and Paul.
 3. Mr Coopers shop is in the High Street.
 4. Mens shirts are sold here.
 5. We went to a party at Carols house.
 6. The monkeys cage was too small for them.
 7. I borrowed my friends book.
 8. There were many letters in the postmans bag.
 9. There were lovely childrens books in the shop.
10. Stories endings are not always happy.

B. The words in brackets ( ) in each of these sentences needs either **'s** or **'** after it. Write out the sentences as they should be.

1. Mr (Lewis) dog is a terrier.
2. I saw Mr (Morris) car outside school.
3. (Elephants) tusks are made of ivory.
4. Seven (babies) cots were in a row.
5. My (class) attendance is good.
6. Many (countries) athletes take part in the Olympic Games.
7. We searched for Mrs (Greens) glasses.
8. Hay was put in all the (horses) stables.
9. (Denis) birthday is in September.
10. (Fairies) wings are made of gossamer.

15. The apostrophe for words that are shortened

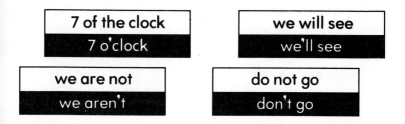

They're sure to be late.
We'll meet you in the park.
School finishes at **4 o'clock**.

When we speak, we often run words together and cut them short. The words in **dark print** above are examples.

When we write these words, **we use the apostrophe (') to show where a letter or letters have been missed out.**

I ~~am~~ going.
I'm going.

We did n~~o~~t wait.
We didn't wait.

For you to do:

A. Write out the sentences below, and put in the apostrophe
to show where a letter or letters have been missed out.

1. Weve a big dog at home.
2. They didnt help us much.
3. I hope itll be a fine day tomorrow.
4. The story wasnt a funny one.
5. He cant see that his sum is wrong.
6. Were sending Tom a present for Christmas.
7. She wouldnt play with my doll.
8. Dont forget to post my letter.
9. Hell soon be coming back.
10. We hadnt a long way to go.

B. Write out these sentences, using a short form for the words
underlined.

1. I <u>have not</u> been to the circus.
2. They <u>were not</u> afraid of the dog.
3. You <u>should not</u> play with fire.
4. It <u>is not</u> far to walk.
5. <u>It is</u> a pity you lost your ball.
6. <u>She is</u> coming to play with me.
7. He <u>could not</u> see where he was going.
8. I hope <u>you will</u> have a good time.
9. <u>You have</u> kept your book very tidy.
10. <u>That is</u> the way to the park.

C. Write out the top row of words, and under each pair put
its short form. The short forms are in the bottom row, but
they are not in the correct order.

they have	who would	who will	does not	do not
who'd	don't	doesn't	they've	who'll

16. Question marks

 What is the time?
How old are you?
Where is he going?

A sentence that asks something is called a question. There are three questions above.

Always start a question with a capital letter, and end with a question mark (?).

For you to do:

A. Write out these questions correctly, putting in the capital letters and the question marks.

1. what train shall you catch
2. how far is it to London
3. when can you see me
4. where shall we go today
5. why did I send him away
6. who painted this picture
7. is your sum right
8. can you tell me the way
9. do you like ice cream
10. shall we go for a walk

B. Here are some sentences and some questions. Write them all out and put in the full stops and question marks that have been left out.

1. Have you ever been to the zoo
2. All sorts of wild animals are kept there
3. Some are kept in cages
4. Do you know the names of any animals that are kept in cages
5. Lions and tigers are kept in cages.
6. What animals in a zoo can roam about outside the cages
7. Usually elephants and camels do this
8. What work do the elephants do
9. Very often they give rides to children

17. Commas to separate **yes** and **no**

Question.   Have you a pet?
Answer.   **Yes,** I have a dog.
Question.   Are you wet?
Answer.   **No,** it is not raining.

Look at the answers to the questions.

When YES and NO are used in answers to questions, a comma separates them from the rest of the sentence.

Do you know the time?
No, I haven't a watch.

Comma after **No,** because this is an answer.

There are no pictures in my book.

No comma, because this is not an answer.

43

For you to do:

A. Each of these sentences needs a comma. Write out the sentences and put in the comma where it should be.

1. No he was early for school this morning.
2. Yes I saw him in the street.
3. Yes I should like to come to your party.
4. No she stayed at home all day.
5. Yes we read it last year.
6. No they went the other way.

B. Some of these sentences require a comma. Others do not. Write out the sentences which require a comma, and put the comma in the correct place.

1. There are no wolves in England now.
2. Yes if you will lend me your ball.
3. She is no longer my friend.
4. No I am going to a music lesson.
5. Yes of course I can.
6. We have no boys in our school.
7. No one is allowed in the park after dark.
8. There is no time to play with your toys now.
9. Yes I shall be very glad to help you.
10. No seven of them were wrong.

18. Exclamation marks

If you sit on a pin, you cry out—**Oh!**
If you are drowning, you shout—**Help!**
If you receive a birthday present you probably say—**What a lovely present!**

Often, when we have strong feelings about anything, we cry out, or exclaim, in our excitement, something like the words in **dark print** above.

The words we exclaim, which show pain, fear, pleasure, anger, joy or surprise are called exclamations.

An exclamation need not be a sentence, but it must always start with a capital letter, and end with an exclamation mark (!).

For you to do:

A. Below are six exclamations. Write them out, and put in the capital letters and exclamation marks.

1. stop thief
2. what a beautiful house
3. oh dear
4. good gracious
5. how cold the weather is
6. you poor child

B. Some of these are sentences, and some are exclamations. Write out the exclamations and put in the capital letters, full stops and exclamation marks.

1. he sat down with a bump
2. let me go
3. oh heavens
4. i spoke to their mother
5. how tired he looks
6. get out of my way
7. what a joke
8. i hope it will stop raining

Revision test 3A

A. Put an apostrophe **'** or **'s** in each of these sentences where
required.

1. An ass ears are long and pointed.
2. Joannas father is a farmer.
3. The sheeps wool is used for making clothes.
4. Wholl come to the pictures?
5. I met James mother.
6. Gladys gloves were lost in the bus.
7. We arent tired yet.
8. The knifes edge was blunt.
9. A womens meeting was held in the hall.
10. I have my tea at five oclock.
11. The palaces windows were broken.
12. Many peoples holidays are very short.
13. We went for a ride in Mr Longs car.
14. He hasnt told me his name.

B. Some of the following are questions, and the rest are
exclamations. Write them out correctly, using capital
letters and the punctuation mark required.

1. bravo
2. how far is it to london
3. what a fine day it is
4. can you see the house from here
5. how old is eric
6. how old he looks
7. what will you do when you grow up
8. be off with you
9. fire fire
10. do you know what he wants

Revision test 3B

No capital letters or punctuation marks have been used in these groups of sentences. Write out each group of sentences, and put in all the capital letters and punctuation marks that are needed.

1. look out here comes father christmas its christmas eve december 24 and hes driving his sledge across the roof tops its piled high with dolls crackers engines and all kinds of toys alice mary frank jimmy and hundreds of other children are lying asleep and dreaming of full and exciting stockings that they will be able to explore on christmas day

2. have you heard of rip van winkle he lived near the catskill mountains in america he didnt like work and his wife mrs rip van winkle was always calling him a lazy wretch one day rip wandered up the hillside near his home and took a nap that lasted 20 years when he awoke he returned to his village at first no one knew who he was

3. mr and mrs brown moved to 25 north road oxbridge on wednesday 30 march 1973 before that they had lived at 16 green avenue brisdon for twelve years mr browns work was in an office their childrens names were angela michael and denis when they got to oxbridge all the children went to south street primary school where the headmaster was mr harris

4. having seen teresa safely on the bus i hurried to my friends house in devon lane she has a dog a dear little creature called pip which we often take for walks in manor park pip races about chases a ball runs after stones searches for rabbits and thoroughly enjoys himself so do teresa and i

5. mary stopped in front of the shop opened her purse and took out twenty pence then she gazed in the window there were chocolates toffees gums and peppermints when she had made up her mind she walked into the shop lucky mary

19. Quotation marks for speech (1)

Jim speaks. | There is a circus in town. |

Jim says, "There is a circus in town."

In the top line above the words that Jim actually used have been put in a box to keep them apart from *Jim speaks*.

When we write the two sentences, as we have done in the second line, we do not use a box, but put quotation marks to show what was in the box.

In the same way:

Ken speaks. | It would be fun to see it. |

Ken says, "It would be fun to see it."

Quotation, or speech, marks (" ") are used in writing to show words that have been spoken.

Only words actually spoken must be put inside quotation marks. The first word inside the quotation marks begins with a capital letter.

There must always be two punctuation marks between an ordinary sentence (Jim says) and the words actually spoken by anyone (in the box).

In the sentences above the two marks are ,"

For you to do:

A. Write out these sentences and put in the quotation and other punctuation marks that are needed.

1. Sue told me We will go to the pictures together

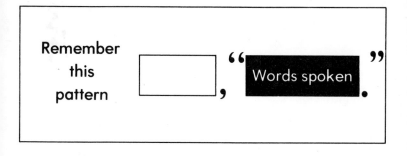

Remember this pattern ⸢ ⸣ , " Words spoken ".

2. Mr Short whispered Don't make any noise
3. Robert said I wish I could ride your bicycle
4. Mr Chapman remarked There are some fine potatoes in my garden
5. My mother called It is raining
6. Carol cried Don't cross the road without me
7. Simon shouted I can see where you are
8. Mrs Morton said The shops are all crowded today
9. Ruth said My doll needs a new dress
10. William boasted I am the tallest boy in the class

B. No capital letters or punctuation marks have been used in these sentences. Write out the sentences and put in all the capital letters, punctuation, and quotation marks that should have been used.

1. Steven cried i have lost a pound
2. mr hunt complained there is no sugar in my tea
3. oliver reported i saw two cars collide
4. mr young called you must hurry up
5. the postman said please sign on this line
6. the conductor told me i have no change for a pound note
7. the grocer said we have no biscuits today
8. mother said the lady is coming here this morning
9. sarah remarked it is time for me to go to bed
10. jenny sobbed he has broken my doll

20. Quotation marks for speech (2)

| I am in the top class. | Jane speaks. |

"I am in the top class,"   says Jane.

| So am I. | Jill speaks. |

"So am I,"   says Jill.

In these sentences we have changed the order. Look at the punctuation. **Quotation marks are used to show what words were actually spoken:** that is, the words in the boxes. The full stop in the boxes becomes a comma, because the sentence in the box is connected with the ordinary sentence.

Should there be a comma before *says*?

No, because we already have two punctuation marks to separate the sentences: ,"

Remember this pattern   " Words spoken , " ⬚ .

For you to do:

A. Write out these sentences and put in the quotation marks and other punctuation marks that are needed.

1. We shall be late for dinner said Patrick
2. I wish I could have some more pudding grumbled Colin
3. There are some fine trees in the park remarked Mr King
4. Tony has broken my doll cried Sally
5. I have won the prize announced Ned
6. We are learning to dance said Ruth and Mary
7. Six fives are thirty stated the teacher

8. Cross the road and turn to the right said the policeman
9. Run if you want to catch the train advised the porter
10. Come in at once called Mother

B. No capital letters or punctuation marks have been used in these sentences. Write out the sentences and put in all the capital letters, punctuation, and quotation marks that should have been used.

1. bring your own cup and saucer said brenda
2. i should take the bus if i were you suggested mr ford
3. show mr gray what you have done said the teacher
4. all the boys are over ten remarked mrs long
5. leave the door open when you go out said leslie
6. dig as deep as you can advised the gardener
7. choose which one you want said father
8. you cannot catch me shouted the boy
9. only two more seats left announced the manager
10. here are my sums said clare

21. Quotation marks for speech (3)

Bill speaks. | What a lovely day it is! |

Bill says,   "What a lovely day it is!"

Jim speaks. | Are you going for a walk? |

Jim says,   "Are you going for a walk?"

The sentences above show one way of writing questions and exclamations in quotation marks.

Always put the question or exclamation mark inside the quotation marks.

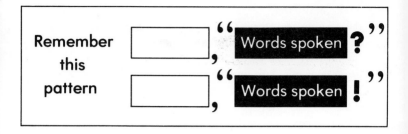

For you to do:

A. The quotation marks and some of the punctuation marks have been missed out of these sentences. Write out the sentences and put in the quotation marks and any other punctuation marks that are required.

1. Joe asked What is the time?
2. Ian begged Will you please help me with my work?
3. The bather screamed Help!
4. Liza asked Will you buy a ticket for a concert?
5. Fay exclaimed What a lovely dress!
6. Mrs Taylor asked Have you any butter today?
7. The man exclaimed Look out!
8. The conductor asked How far are you going?
9. The tramp asked Can you spare 5p?
10. The lady cried How wet it is!

B. No capital letters or punctuation have been put in these sentences. Write out the sentences and put in all the capital letters, punctuation marks, and quotation marks that are needed.

1. mr jones exclaimed rubbish
2. the boy begged will you please let me go with the others
3. miss baker asked did you see the crowd outside
4. the crowd yelled goal

5. mr williams inquired why did you lock the door
6. the prisoner pleaded can i see my wife
7. mother exclaimed for goodness sake wash yourself
8. the queen shouted off with his head
9. the manager inquired is dr groves here
10. the policeman asked where are you going

22. Quotation marks for speech (4)

| What a lovely book this is! | Mary speaks.

"What a lovely book this is!" says Mary.

| Will you let me read it? | Fay speaks.

"Will you let me read it?" says Fay.

Here is another way of putting questions and exclamations in quotation marks.

When the punctuation in the box is a question mark or exclamation mark, it is not changed.

The mark must be put inside the quotation marks.

Notice that we still use two punctuation marks between the speech and the ordinary sentence: **!"** *or* **?"**.

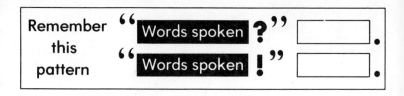

Remember this pattern

" Words spoken ?" [ ] .
" Words spoken !" [ ] .

For you to do:

A. The quotation marks and some punctuation marks have been missed out of these sentences. Write out the sentences and put in the quotation marks and any other punctuation marks that are needed.

1. Do you remember where you put it? asked Father
2. Good gracious! exclaimed the gentleman
3. What an awful sight you are! my mother exclaimed
4. How can I go to the pictures? asked Julie
5. Shoot! yelled the crowd
6. What is your name? demanded the policeman
7. Why are you crying? asked the lady
8. What a huge lake! gasped the traveller
9. Can we go to the seaside? begged Alan
10. Who is the captain of the team? asked the referee

B. No capital letters or punctuation marks have been used in these sentences. Write out the sentences and put in all the capital letters, punctuation marks, and quotation marks that should have been used.

1. what have you been doing asked nick
2. do you like a holiday in the country helen asked
3. what a lovely horse exclaimed denis
4. how do you know that inquired the postman
5. have you been to the circus this year mr green inquired
6. off with you shouted the farmer
7. have you any brothers or sisters asked tim
8. how tired i am sighed kate
9. how long have you been at school asked the teacher
10. what a fine sunset michael exclaimed

23. Quotation marks for speech (5)

| I have to stay in, so that I can help Mother. | Joan speaks.

| I have to stay in, | Joan speaks. | so that I can help Mother. |

"I have to stay in," says Joan, "so that I can help Mother."

As the sentence in the box is so long, we can split it into two.

No changes are made to words or punctuation in the box, but the full stop after _Joan speaks_ becomes a comma.

This is because the two boxes contain only one long sentence, and it would be wrong to have a full stop anywhere between them.

Remember this pattern "Words," [ ], "spoken."

For you to do:

A. The quotation marks and other punctuation marks have been left out of these sentences. Write out the sentences, and put in all the punctuation marks that are required.

1. There is not much time left said Bill and there is a great deal to do.

2. I went to the seaside last year said Bob but I am going to the country this year

3. If you put sugar in water explained the teacher it will dissolve
4. When you get back home said Mother you must dry your clothes
5. I fell over cried Cathy and I have cut my knee
6. This is the house explained the postman but no one lives here now
7. Come in very quietly whispered Mrs Freeman for the baby is asleep
8. I am tired of rice pudding grumbled Joe because we have it every day
9. While you were out said my brother Philip called to see you
10. If you are a good boy said my aunt I will give you a chocolate

B. No capital letters or punctuation marks have been used in these sentences. Write out the sentences and put in all the capital letters, quotation marks and other punctuation marks that should have been used.

1. when i have finished my work said lily i can come out to play
2. we have still three kilometres to go grumbled the soldier and it is nearly dark
3. while you are away eva said remember to send me a postcard
4. you must not play with fire my father warned me or you will get burned
5. a hundred years explained the teacher is called a century
6. it has been freezing so hard said the park-keeper that you can skate on the pond
7. if you do not put some coal on the fire mother said it will go out
8. when i have written this letter said my brother i want you to post it
9. this book is most exciting paul said and i shall be sorry when i have finished it
10. i will give you 10p promised the old lady if you will help me to carry this parcel

24. Quotation marks for speech (6)

| I must be at school before 9. Is it time to go? | Peter speaks.

| I must be at school before 9. | Peter speaks. | Is it time to go? |

"I must be at school before 9," says Peter. "Is it time to go?"

This looks as if we have broken one of the rules. Why is there a full stop after *Peter* in line 3? Why not a comma?

There are two sentences in the first long box in line 1. In line 2, the second box starts a new sentence, and begins with a capital letter.

The full stop after *Peter* is used to show that there are two separate sentences in the quotation marks.

| What is the time? I must be at school before 9. | Mary speaks.

| What is the time? | Mary speaks. | I must be at school before 9. |

"What is the time?" says Mary."I must be at school before 9."

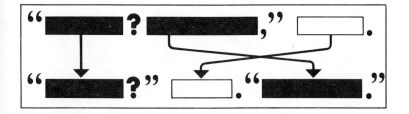

For you to do:
A. All the punctuation marks have been missed out of these

57

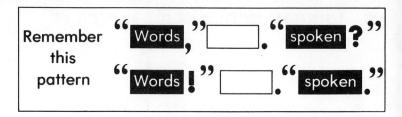

Remember this pattern

"Words," [ ]. "spoken?"

"Words!" [ ]. "spoken."

sentences. Write the sentences out and put in the quotation marks and any other punctuation marks that are required.

1. I cannot be bothered drawled Terry It is far too hot
2. Have you seen Kate asked Judith She has my coat
3. I am going to the Town Hall said Mr Martin Can you please tell me the way
4. Hurrah cried Simon I have found my ball
5. I have not touched your boys protested Dan What an idea
6. Halt shouted the sentry Who goes there
7. Good gracious exclaimed the teacher What is this
8. Oh dear sighed Mrs Ellis I wish I could find the scissors
9. You beast said Jane Have you eaten my toffee
10. You are looking very pale said the doctor Do you feel ill

B. No capital letters or punctuation marks have been used in these sentences. Write out the sentences and put in all the capital letters, quotation marks, and other punctuation marks that should have been used.

1. ouch shouted the boy that hurt
2. why did you give your stamps away asked sam were you tired of collecting them
3. do you help your mother asked anne i always wash up
4. oh dear sobbed the little girl i have broken my doll
5. look out exclaimed the man there is a car coming
6. i have 50p said the boy have you
7. what an old hat said jean are you going to wear it
8. stop that noise called mother baby is asleep
9. where is my book enquired aunt eva i put it on the chair
10. a hundred pennies make one pound said the teacher how much do a hundred halfpennies make

58

25. Quotation marks for speech (7)

"Where have you been?" asked Mother.

"I went swimming in the river," Tommy answered.

"Good gracious!" exclaimed his father. "That's very dangerous. You might be drowned."

"Mind you don't do it again," said Mother.

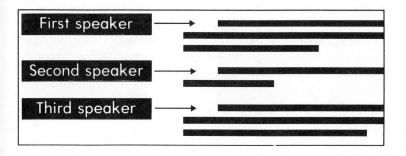

When you are writing what a number of people have said, as in the sentences above, remember this rule: **Start a fresh paragraph for each new speaker**.

For you to do:

A. The punctuation marks have been missed out of these sentences. Write out the sentences, and put in the quotation marks and other punctuation marks that are required. Remember to start a fresh paragraph for each new speaker.

1. What is the time asked Jane Seven o'clock Mother replied
2. I have a stamp album said Jerry So have I said Frank
3. Oh shouted the man What is the matter asked his friend
4. Is this the way asked Clare Yes answered the policeman
5. Give me one of your sweets said Jimmy Why should I asked Neil You have a bagful replied Jimmy

B. No punctuation marks or capital letters have been used in these sentences. Write out the sentences, and put in the capital letters, quotation marks and other punctuation marks that are required. Remember to start a fresh paragraph for each new speaker.

1. what a lovely morning exclaimed jenny i am going to play in the park i wish i could come with you said mary but i have to go to the shops
2. would you like to come to my party asked simon i would love to replied philip when is it
3. how old are you asked the teacher i am nine answered jill when shall you be ten asked the teacher next june said jill
4. why did the chicken cross the road asked chris i dont know said bob to get to the other side laughed chris
5. what time does the train leave for bristol asked mr grant eight oclock replied the porter good gracious exclaimed mr grant i have got to wait an hour and a half

26. Quotation marks for titles

We saw **"Cinderella"** at the theatre.
"The Daffodils" is a well-known poem.
I have read four chapters of **"Ivanhoe"**.

The words in **dark print** are titles.

When you write the titles of books, plays, films or poems in sentences, put quotation marks around them.

The first word in a title, and all other important words, begin with capital letters.

For you to do:

A. In each of these sentences is a title. Write out the sentences, and put in the capital letters and quotation marks that should have been used.

1. hiawatha is a poem about a Red Indian boy.
2. black beauty is the story of a horse written by Anna Sewell.
3. The life of black slaves was described in uncle tom's cabin.
4. Lewis Carroll wrote alice in wonderland. He also wrote alice through the looking glass.
5. the wind in the willows is a fine story about animals.
6. I enjoyed reading robinson crusoe.
7. Shakespeare wrote a play called as you like it.
8. the three musketeers is an exciting adventure film.
9. I read motoring world every month.
10. This book is called exercises in punctuation.

B. Write one sentence to answer each of these questions.

1. What is the title of the last book you read?
2. What pantomime would you like to see most?
3. What is the title of the film you most enjoyed?
4. What arithmetic book do you use in school?
5. What poem can you say by heart?

C. In the first column are the names of authors. In the second column is the title of a book the author wrote, though the title is not written correctly. For each author and title, write a sentence like the example given. Make sure that you write the titles correctly.

Author	*Title of book*
Charles Dickens	david copperfield

Example: Charles Dickens wrote "David Copperfield".

R. L. Stevenson	treasure island
John Ruskin	the king of the golden river
Charles Kingsley	the water babies
Hans Andersen	the ugly duckling
Charles Dickens	oliver twist

Sir W. Scott	ivanhoe
Fenimore Cooper	the last of the mohicans
John Bunyan	pilgrim's progress

Charles Dickens wrote "David Copperfield", "Oliver Twist", "Pickwick Papers" and other novels.

I have read "Black Beauty", "Treasure Island" and "Footprints in the Forest" this term.

When you write a list of titles in a sentence, put each title in quotation marks, and separate the titles by commas unless the word 'and' already separates them. (See Lesson 9.)

The commas are put *outside* **the quotation marks.**

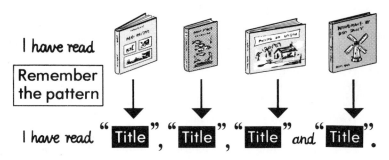

I have read

Remember the pattern

I have read "Title", "Title", "Title" and "Title".

For you to do:

A. Each of these sentences contains a list of titles. Write out the sentences correctly, putting in capital letters, quotation marks and any other punctuation marks required.

1. At the pictures last month I saw the sting the three musketeers and robin hood

2. Shakespeare wrote twelfth night hamlet the tempest and other plays

3. mother goose aladdin and puss in boots are three pantomimes I have seen

4. dawn sea fever and the west wind are three poems by John Masefield

5. Dumas wrote the three musketeers the queens necklace twenty years after and many other novels

27. The pattern of a letter

Dear Bill I am going camping in 3 days' time I have a tent and everything is arranged. I should like you to come with me. Can you? Please let me know & I will tell you what you must take Your old friend Jim

Poor Bill! Of course he'd like to go camping with Jim, but how can he reply? Jim hasn't told him his address, and Bill doesn't even know exactly when Jim is going away. Jim says in three days' time, but when is that? It depends when Jim wrote the letter, and he hasn't put the date.

And what an untidy letter! Perhaps you don't think this is important, but it does help to be able to see at a glance who a letter is for and who wrote it.

So that all letters shan't be a muddle like this one, **there is a special way of setting down a letter so that nothing important is missed out, and so that you can see at a glance what it's about.**

We might call this special way of setting it down the **pattern of a letter**. This pattern is shown on the next page.

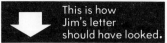

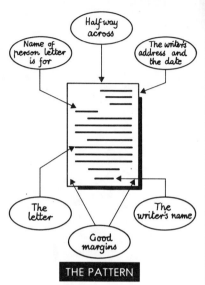

THE PATTERN

43 High St,
Watford
1 Jan., 1975

Dear Bill,
I am going camping in
3 days' time. I have a tent
and everything is arranged.
I should like you to come
with me. Can you? Please let
me know and I will tell you
what we must take.
Your old friend,
Jim

Look carefully at the punctuation marks on the letter Jim
should have written, particularly at those in the first 4 lines and
last 2 lines on the paper. These marks should always be used when
you are writing a letter.

Here are some addresses and dates written out, so that you
can see the punctuation exactly:

29 Cambey St,
Hyton,
Surrey.
May 3, 1976

The Nook,
Main Road,
Oxbridge
1 June 1976

For you to do:

Here are some very muddled letters. Some of the punctuation has been missed out, and none of them follow the pattern of a letter. Write them out properly as letters, using the pattern you have been shown, and putting in the punctuation required.

1. 25 King Street York 12 February 1975 dear Liz I was sorry to hear that you have had an accident and that you are in hospital. I hope you will soon be better. We all look forward to seeing you back at school. Best wishes Linda.

2. 38 Bull Lane Preston 22 November 1976 dear Mr Lay I am sorry that Peter cannot come to school today but he has a bad cold. I will send him as soon as he is better. Yours truly Mrs A. James.

3. The Gables Howard Road Gloucester 15 April 1973 dear Stephen Thank you very much for your birthday card. I had many lovely presents which I will show you next Saturday. Mind you get here by half past two. Best wishes from Philip.

4. 112 Thornton Avenue Dover 20 December 1974 dear Jane I would like you to come to my Christmas party which I am having on Saturday December 28. Please let me know if you are able to come. The party starts at 3 o'clock. Love from Lorna.

5. 17 Hope Street Manchester 19 May 1975 dear Mr Lewis Your suit is now ready and I should be glad if you would call here to have it fitted as soon as you can. We close each day at half past five. Yours Sincerely J. Robinson.

28. The pattern of an envelope

A letter has a pattern.
So has the address on an envelope.
Is there any need for this? There certainly is.

Every day hundreds of thousands of envelopes have to be sorted in post offices, and it makes the sorter's job much easier and quicker if all the envelopes are addressed in good, clear writing, and in the same pattern.

First of all, look to your writing. Secondly, remember the **pattern for the address** on the envelope:

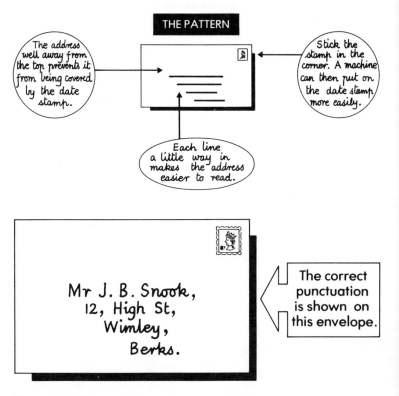

THE PATTERN

The address well away from the top prevents it from being covered by the date stamp.

Stick the stamp in the corner. A machine can then put on the date stamp more easily.

Each line a little way in makes the address easier to read.

Mr J. B. Snook,
12, High St,
Wimley,
Berks.

The correct punctuation is shown on this envelope.

For you to do:

A. Here are some names and addresses with the punctuation marks missed out. Write each name and address as you would do on an envelope, using the punctuation marks that are needed, and following the pattern you have been shown.

1. Mr G A Farr 53 Lanark St Glossop Derby
2. Rev B Rank The Haven 18 Holland Ave Bruton Avon

3. Mr and Mrs O G Davies 116 Easterfield Lane Malton Yorks
4. Dr R W Stokes The Elms 71 Tudor St Epping Essex
5. Mrs A Lee 95 Maclean Rd Parkgate Cheshire
6. Mr K Brown The Cedars High View Retford Notts
7. Dr S M Martin 146 Kingswood Gdns Ware Herts
8. Miss P Cooper Rosebank Green Lane Cobham Surrey
9. Mr S E Lewis 153 Riverside Cres Tenby Pembs
10. Rev W Young 45 Valley Ave Leek Staffs

B. Address envelopes to:
1. Your father.
2. Your teacher.
3. Your grocer.
4. Your best friend.
5. One of your cousins.

Revision test 4A

A. The quotation marks and other punctuation marks have been missed out of these sentences. Write out the sentences as they should be. Remember the paragraphs.

1. Can you help me with these sums asked George I'm sorry I can't Tom answered because I have to do my own

2. Mother asked Where did you put the cake In the cupboard answered Emma I can't see it said Mother Perhaps Daddy has taken it suggested Emma

3. Good gracious said teacher You do look dirty I slipped in the mud explained Robert The teacher said You had better go and wash yourself

4. Will you tell me asked the man where I can find the post office Take the first turn right and the second turn left I replied Thank you said the man

5. Look cried Ronald Here comes the fire engine There must be a fire shouted Jack Yes I can see the smoke Shall we go and watch the firemen asked Ronald Oh yes cried Jack I should love to

B. Here are some letters that have not been written properly. write them out as they ought to be.

1. 43 Station Road Margate 29 March 1975 dear Miss Small Could you please make a dress for my daughter? I have the material and shall be in after 3 o'clock every afternoon next week. Will you please call? Yours sincerely B. Goodwin

2. 85 Mill Crescent Swansea 8 Sept 1976 dear sir Will you please send me one of the stamp albums you advertised in your magazine? I enclose a postal order for 75p. Yours faithfully Eric Edwards.

3. 12 Windmill Street Southend 30 August 1973 dear Marion I have been here with Mum and Dad for a week now and we are having a lovely holiday. We haven't had a drop of rain and I have played on the sands every day. I have had lots of donkey rides and yesterday I saw the Punch and Judy Show. There are crowds of people here love from Sue

4. 126 Court Lane Bidchester 27 April 1976 dear Lynn Thank you for your letter. I should like to go to the pictures next Wednesday. I will meet you at the Town Hall at 6 o'clock. Best wishes Anne.

5. The Gables Clarke Road Crantall 15 October 1972 dear Frank Thank you for lending me Robinson Crusoe. I have enjoyed reading it very much. Wouldn't it be fun to be wrecked on a desert island and do everything that Crusoe did? Yours Tim.

Revision test 4B

Rewrite the following, putting in all capital letters and punctuation marks that are needed.

1. so he took leave of his friend with many thanks groped his way out as well as he could into the now lamp-lighted streets and hurried off to get his dinner

2. gone not a sound could i hear but the blowing of a fish now and then on the surface of the sea and the creak of the brigs crazy old spars as she rolled gently from side to side with the little swell there was on the quiet water

3. at michaelmas in the year 1776 my dear and kind friend doctor barnard having to go to london with his rents proposed to take me to london to see my other patron sir peter denis between whom and the doctor there was a great friendship

4. things dangle from the vessels stern as did weapons from the knight in through the looking glass among them are nets full of vegetables many noisy fowls in a wicker basket certain boxes spare oars and a few china pots with flowers

5. the next day i left marsh end for morton the day after diana and mary quitted it for distant boughton in a week mr rivers and hannah repaired to the parsonage and so the old grange was abandoned

6. we played with flags i said flags echoed my sister yes said i estella waved a blue flag and i waved a red one and miss havisham waved one sprinkled all over with little gold stars out at the coach-window and then we all waved our swords and hurrahed swords repeated my sister where did you get swords from out of a cupboard said i

7. on christmas day in the year 1642 isaac newton was born at the small village of woolsthorpe in lincolnshire little did his mother think when she beheld her new-born babe that he was destined to explain many matters which had been a mystery ever since the creation of the world isaacs father being dead mrs newton was married again to a clergyman and went to reside at north witham

8. but the windows are patched with wooden panes and the door i think is like the gate it is never opened how it would groan and grate against the stone floor if it were for it is a solid heavy handsome door

9. the clouds quickly cleared away and the western sun soon shone out bright and clear full in the faces of the french at length the genoese bowmen drew their arblasts and commenced their discharge and each english archer stepped forward a single pace as he took his bow from the case in which it had been protected from the rain a flight of arrows fell among the genoese piercing their heads arms and faces and causing them instantly to retreat in confusion among the horsemen in their rear

10. have some wine the march hare said in an encouraging tone alice looked all round the table but there was nothing on it but tea i dont see any wine she remarked there isnt any said the march hare then it wasnt very civil of you to offer it said alice angrily it wasnt very civil of you to sit down without being invited said the march hare i didnt know it was your table said alice its laid for a great many more than three

11. the skipper was on deck with two of our best men for watch the rest were below except the pilot who coiled himself up more like a snake than a man on the forecastle it was not my watch till four in the morning but i didnt like the look of the night or the pilot or the state of things generally and i shook myself down on deck to get my nap there and be ready for anything at a moments notice the last i remember was the skipper whispering to me that he didnt like the look of things either and that he would go below and consult his instructions

12. hallo growled scrooge what do you mean by coming here at this time of day im very sorry sir said bob i am behind my time you are repeated scrooge yes i think you are step this way if you please its only once a year sir pleaded bob it shall not be repeated i was making rather merry yesterday sir

13. what splendid weather it is said he to himself this wind goes fairly through and through me and makes me feel so strong that i quite crackle all over what i wonder is that fiery red thing hanging in the sky it neednt stare at me it wont make me blink ill stare it out of countenance and he watched the sun as it slowly sank down in the west

14. i have no time to pause for meat or drink said he i have a long journey to make before morning in what direction said i andalusia said he exactly my route said i so as you wont stop and eat with me perhaps you will let me mount and ride with you i see your horse is of a powerful frame ill warrant hell carry double agreed said the trooper

15. you are not particularly attached to it i daresay said mr pickwick trembling with anxiety you wouldnt mind selling it no ah but whod buy it inquired the man with an expression of face which he probably meant to be very cunning ill give give you ten shillings for it at once said mr pickwick if you would take it up for me

16. he is not here sir replied nicholas dont tell me a lie retorted the schoolmaster he is he is not retorted nicholas angrily dont tell me one we shall soon see that said mr squeers rushing upstairs ill find him i warrant you

17. is tommy chapman the apothecarys son of westgate alive yet and does he remember my wagging my head to him as our chaise whirled by he was shaking a mat at the door of his fathers shop as my lordship accompanied by my noble friend passed by

18. have you had a bad night maam asked nell i seldom have anything else child replied mrs jarley with the air of a martyr i sometimes wonder how i bear it

19. isaacs playmates were enchanted with his new windmill they thought that nothing so pretty and so wonderful had ever been seen in the whole world but isaac said one of them you have forgotten one thing that belongs to a mill what is that asked isaac for he supposed that from the roof of the mill to its foundation he had forgotten nothing why where is the miller said his friend that is true i must look out for one said isaac

20. johnsons horse had also been brought and its rider had some trouble in mounting you will delay me sir if you insist on keeping me company said alastair i am a strong rider when i am once in the saddle said the other humbly but why this hurry you will be in derby long ere daybreak i do not ride to derby but down the vale to overtake a certain gentleman